animals**animals**

Jaguars
by **Steven Otfinoski**

mc Marshall Cavendish
Benchmark

New York

Special thanks to Donald E. Moore III, associate director of animal care at the Smithsonian Institution's National Zoo, for his expert reading of this manuscript.

Published by Marshall Cavendish Benchmark
An imprint of Marshall Cavendish Corporation

Other Marshall Cavendish Offices:
Marshall Cavendish International (Asia) Private Limited, 1 New Industrial Road, Singapore 536196 • Marshall Cavendish International (Thailand) Co Ltd. 253 Asoke, 12th Flr, Sukhumvit 21 Road, Klongtoey Nua, Wattana, Bangkok 10110, Thailand • Marshall Cavendish (Malaysia) Sdn Bhd, Times Subang, Lot 46, Subang Hi-Tech Industrial Park, Batu Tiga, 40000 Shah Alam, Selangor Darul Ehsan, Malaysia
Marshall Cavendish is a trademark of Times Publishing Limited

All websites were available and accurate when this book was sent to press.

Library of Congress Cataloging-in-Publication Data
Otfinoski, Steven.
Jaguars / by Steven Otfinoski.
p. cm. — (Animals animals)
Includes index.
Summary: "Provides comprehensive information on the anatomy, special skills, habitats, and diet of jaguars"—Provided by publisher.
ISBN 978-0-7614-4839-6
1. Jaguar—Juvenile literature. I. Title.
QL737.C23O22 2011
599.75'5—dc22
2009022627

Photo research by Joan Meisel

Cover photo: Demetrio Carrasco/Getty Images

The photographs in this book are used by permission and through the courtesy of:
Alamy: Mark Bowler, 20; Bruce Coleman Brakefield, 24; Peter Arnold, Inc., 26; Stock Connection Blue, 33; Martin Spragg/Art Directors, 37; Terry Whittaker, 39. *Corbis*: DLILLC, 16; Barnabas Bosshart, 34. *Getty Images*: Steve Winter, 1; DEA/G. Dagli Orti, 4; Carol Farneti-Foster, 6; Burke/Triolo Productions, 7; Peter Arnold, Inc., 9; Jeff Foott, 10, 32; Peter Lilja, 19; James Balog, 22; WireImage, 27; Thomas Schmitt, 30; Samba Photos/Paulo Fridman, 38; Jonathan Booth, 40. *Minden Pictures*: SA Team/Foto Natura, 25, 28. *Peter Arnold, Inc.*: TUNS, 13; Luiz C. Marigo, 14; BIOS Bios-Auteurs Cavignaus Regis, 15; Biosphoto/Klein J.-L. & Hubert M.-L., 21.

Editor: Joy Bean
Publisher: Michelle Bisson
Art Director: Anahid Hamparian
Series Designer: Adam Mietlowski

Printed in Malaysia (T)
135642

Contents

1 One Powerful Cat

Few animals have captured the imagination of people as much as the jaguar. The ancient Olmecs of what is now Mexico worshiped the jaguar as a god. The Aztecs, who later lived in Mexico, had a god named Tezcatlipoca who took the form of a jaguar. For certain tribes in the Amazon River region of Brazil, the jaguar was an evil spirit with great power. People still admire the jaguar's strength and courage today. For example, one of the fastest and sleekest of sports cars is named the Jaguar.

The jaguar is one of four large wild cats that humans have never *domesticated*. The other three are the lion, the tiger, and the leopard. Together, those

A statue of a jaguar god from the Olmec civilization of ancient Mexico.

The jaguar is one of four large wild cats in the world.

wild cats are sometimes called the Big Four. A jaguar is smaller than a lion and a tiger but is bigger than most leopards, which are its closest relatives. There are many smaller wild cats around the world, such as the bobcat and the lynx. The jaguar is the only big cat that lives in the *Western Hemisphere*, which includes North, Central, and South America.

The cat family includes both wild cats and the domestic cats we welcome as pets. Domestic cats are distant relatives of wild cats. They are the descendants of the original African wild cat. All cats have

The domestic cat is part of the cat family (Felidae), which the jaguar is also a part of.

long bodies, rounded heads, and powerful jaws with sharp teeth. They are all excellent hunters that kill and eat other animals. One main difference between big cats and smaller cats is that big cats can roar but cannot purr, and small cats can purr but cannot roar.

The jaguar once roamed the American Southwest, including southern California. But shrinking *habitat* and hunters have all but driven this large cat from the United States. Now jaguars are found primarily in parts of Mexico and in Central and South America. Most jaguars live in rain forests and other heavily wooded regions. Some of them thrive on the grasslands of the South American *pampas*, while others manage to survive in dry, semi-desert regions.

Some wild cats avoid water, but not the jaguar. Like tigers, jaguars tend to live near rivers, streams, and lakes. They enjoy swimming and catching fish.

The jaguar has a memorable appearance. It has a coat of golden or brownish-yellow fur covered with black spots and dark rings with markings inside called *rosettes*. Leopards are also spotted. So how do you

Did You Know. . .
Early Native American peoples believed that the skin of the jaguar had magical powers. Warriors would wear the skin of a dead jaguar so that it would give them these powers.

8

The jaguar is a good fisherman and has no problem hunting for food in the water.

The leopard, shown here, has marking that are similar to the jaguar. The leopard's spots are smaller than those of its relative the jaguar, and it has more of them.

tell a jaguar and a leopard apart? There are several important differences. Jaguars' rosettes have small dots inside them, while leopards' rosettes do not. Jaguars are stockier and have a heavier build than leopards. Their tails are thicker, and their heads are larger.

Not all jaguars are golden or brownish in color. Some are black. A black jaguar's coat still has spots and rosettes, but they are harder to see. There are even white jaguars, but they are very rare. Some people call black jaguars or black leopards panthers, but there is really no such animal as a panther. People in earlier times called any black-colored wild cat a panther.

Scientists once thought there were eight *subspecies* of jaguars, which were named after the geographical areas they lived in. In the year 2000, new *genetic* evidence showed there are no true subspecies. All jaguars in the Western Hemisphere are genetically the same. There are, however, small differences in sizes and colorings depending on where the jaguars live. Those are noted in the *species* chart on page 13.

Most jaguars weigh between 124 and 211 pounds (56 and 96 kilograms), but some males can weigh up to 350 pounds (159 kg). Females usually weigh no more than 200 pounds (90 kg) and are smaller than males. Jaguars stand about 27 to 30 inches (69 to 76 centimeters) at the shoulder. A jaguar can be up to 6 feet (1.83 meters) in length with an additional 30 inches (76 cm) of tail.

Species Chart

◆ The Paraná jaguar is the largest of the jaguars. It lives in Argentina and southern Brazil.

A Paraná jaguar.

◆ The Amazon jaguar is found in the forests of the Amazon and Orinoco river basins. It has the darkest fur of any jaguar.

An Amazon jaguar.

◆ The Yucatán jaguar is the smallest of the jaguars. It lives in northern Guatemala and the south-western Yucatán Peninsula, a region of Mexico.

A Yucatán jaguar.

2 Fierce Predator

All the big cats are *carnivores*—animals that eat only the flesh of other animals. Lions and cheetahs chase down their *prey*, but a jaguar relies on the element of surprise. Its fur-covered paws barely make a sound as it roams the forest in search of prey. At the first sight of prey, it stops and remains perfectly still as the other animal approaches. When the target is near enough, the jaguar pounces. What happens next is truly amazing.

The jaguar grasps the animal's body with its forelegs and sinks its sharp teeth between the animal's ears right into its skull. The teeth pierce the prey's brain and kill it almost instantly. The jaguar

Jaguars can leap long distances in order to catch their prey.

has very powerful jaw muscles. It can even bite through the hard shell of a turtle.

Once the prey is dead, the jaguar drags its body to a secluded place and eats it. The jaguar is not a fussy eater. It will devour almost any animal. It prefers large animals such as wild pigs, deer, anacondas (large snakes), caimans (relatives of the alligator), and capybaras (the largest rodents in the world). But jaguars will also eat smaller creatures such as birds, mice, and frogs. Jaguars are also excellent at fishing. They will patiently sit by the water and wait for a fish to swim by. Then they will scoop the fish up with one big paw. Some Native Americans believe the jaguar even dips its tail in the water to attract fish, as a human fisher does with bait on a hook.

A jaguar will hunt whenever it is hungry, night or day. It often has better luck at night, when it can move around under the cover of darkness. The jaguar is the best climber of the big cats. It can climb trees to go after monkeys, sloths, and birds. Sometimes a jaguar will hide on a tree branch and leap down upon prey on the ground. No place is

Did You Know. . .
The word *jaguar* comes from the Indian word *yaguara*, meaning "beast that kills its prey with one bound."

18

Jaguars have long, sharp teeth that help them tear apart their food.

safe for other animals when a hungry jaguar is around!

Jaguars are *solitary* creatures that live and hunt alone. Each animal stakes out its own *territory*, which can range from 2 square miles (5 square kilometers) to 200 square miles (518 square km). As a warning signal to other jaguars, the animal marks the borders of its territory by scratching a tree or squirting urine on the ground. Another jaguar will see the scratches

A black jaguar waits silently before it pounces on its next meal.

Sharp claws help this jaguar climb a tree with ease.

or get one sniff of that powerful scent and will know to stay away.

Jaguars communicate with each other vocally by growling, grunting, or snarling. Some of their grunts sound like coughing and are meant to keep other jaguars away. Unlike lions and tigers, jaguars rarely ever roar.

21

3 Life with Mom

The jaguar is a solitary animal. The only time two jaguars will live together is during mating season, which usually lasts from March to September. Finding a mate in vast areas of land is not easy. Both males and females have developed ways to find and attract a mate. The female jaguar will roam outside her territory and squirt strong-smelling urine on the ground. This lets the male know that she is looking for a mate. The male jaguar will cry out to attract a female. If more than one male meets up with a female in mating season, the strongest male usually scares off weaker ones by roaring loudly. Males rarely fight over a female.

The jaguar spends most of its time alone.

Two mating jaguars are noisy and playful. They roll around and hit at each other with their paws. The male leaves almost immediately after mating takes place. If he should return, the female would most likely drive him away. That prevents him from trying to eat their young when they are born.

A jaguar's pregnancy lasts between 95 and 110 days. When she is ready to give birth, the female looks for a *den*. The den could be a cave, a space underneath a large bush, or even the inside of an abandoned building. The jaguar gives birth to between one and four *cubs* (two cubs is the average). The cubs are about 16 inches (41 cm) long at birth, weigh between 1.5 and 2 pounds (0.7 and 0.9 kg),

Male and female jaguars play around together before mating.

and are blind and helpless. They are born with fur on their bodies, but the markings are different from those of adults. Instead of being clear, the cubs' spots are blotchy and have no rosettes.

After about two weeks, the cubs can open their eyes and see. The only food they eat for about ten weeks is their mother's milk. At six weeks, they are strong enough to accompany their mother on a hunt for food. They learn how and what to hunt by watch-

A young jaguar cub.

ing their mother. At six months, the cubs are ready to hunt on their own, and they start killing and eating small animals. They remain with their mother for a year or two before setting out on their own. By this

A jaguar cub is taken care of by its mother.

Some jaguar cubs are born in zoos and their keepers help to make sure they survive.

time, some females are ready to mate and have children of their own. Males develop more slowly. They are not ready to mate until the age of three or four.

The life span of jaguars in the wild is between twelve and fifteen years. In captivity, however, where there are no natural dangers, jaguars can live as long as twenty-two years. Jaguars are some of the longest-living wild cats.

4 An Adaptable Animal

It is easy to see why early native peoples considered the jaguar a god or a spirit. It is a powerful creature with a muscular body, graceful movements, and a rich, spotted coat. All these qualities are the results of thousands of years of *evolution* and *adaptation* to its environment. The jaguar's stocky, powerful build is made for stalking and pouncing on prey. Its long, sharp teeth and strong jaw muscles are perfect for killing prey with one bite.

Jaguars have adapted to their different environments. Forest-living jaguars are generally smaller than the jaguars living in open grasslands. This may be partly due to the fact that there are fewer large

This jaguar gracefully glides through the water.

animals to prey on in the forests. Rain forests may flood at certain times of the year, and smaller animals can climb into trees more easily. A smaller jaguar can survive in the trees for months if necessary, until the water level goes down.

Sleeping in a tree can help a jaguar stay dry during the rainy season.

The jaguar is adaptable in other ways, too. Although it eats only meat, it eats a wide variety of animals—a total of eighty different species, from cattle and sheep to frogs and birds. The jaguar's keen intelligence helps it to capture prey with as little effort and energy as possible. After stalking an animal, it will wait patiently and spring on it at the right moment. The animal cannot escape.

We admire the jaguar for its beauty and grace, but there are other reasons to admire it. The jaguar helps to protect the *ecosystem* it lives in. By eating many different animals, it helps keep the population of each species under control. If there were too many rodents or wild pigs, they would eat up more than their share of plants and animals, and other species would get crowded out. That would throw off the balance of nature. Many scientists believe the jaguar, the top *predator* in its ecosystem, keeps its environment healthy and balanced with a proper distribution of all the animals in it.

As top predator, the jaguar has little to fear from other animals. A top predator is an animal at the peak of its *food chain*. It eats

Did You Know . . .
We still know very little about jaguars and their behavior. Scientists have had a difficult time observing this highly shy animal in the wild.

other animals, but no animal is capable of killing and eating it. There are no other big cats in the Western Hemisphere to compete with the jaguar for food.

A jaguar stalks its prey.

Jaguars eat a great variety of food, from large cattle to small fish.

Humans are not on the list of creatures the jaguar eats. Jaguar attacks on humans are rare. About the only time a jaguar will attack a person is if it is cornered with no escape route.

The reverse, however, is not true. Humans pose a major threat to jaguars today.

5 Jaguars and People

The jaguar's beauty is one reason why the animal is threatened with extinction. For many years, the jaguar's coat—each one a unique pattern of spots and rosettes—has been a highly prized material for women's jackets, fur coats, and other articles of clothing. By the 1960s and 1970s, about 18,000 jaguars were being killed each year for their coats. Their claws and teeth were also sold as decorative items and souvenirs. It was in danger of becoming *extinct*. The trading of jaguar skins was banned internationally in 1972. The U.S. Fish and Wildlife Service first listed the jaguar as an *endangered* species in 1997. However, illegal hunting of jaguars continues in many Latin American countries today.

Many jaguars have been killed over the years for their fur.

There are other reasons that people hunt and kill jaguars. One is for sport. Another is to protect livestock. As some kinds of prey have disappeared, jaguars have turned to attacking domestic cattle and sheep. Angry ranchers have hunted, trapped, or poisoned jaguars found on their property.

People also kill jaguars because they are afraid of being attacked. When a jaguar is seen near a village or town in the rain forest, the villagers often hunt down and kill the jaguar. Scientists are trying to teach people that jaguars, if left alone, will not bother them.

The biggest threat to jaguars today is environmental change. People in Central and South America are clearing more and more forests and grasslands so they can build farms, homes, towns, and cities. The jaguar's natural territory is rapidly shrinking. The trees that jaguars use to ambush their prey are vanishing. The tall grasses jaguars hide in while stalking animals are dying from *industrial pollution*. As their habitat disappears, so do the animals that jaguars have historically preyed upon.

These threats are serious. Jaguars have already become extinct in El Salvador and in Uruguay. Other countries are sure to follow if we do not take measures to save the jaguar.

How can this be accomplished? The best way may be to create natural *preserves* where jaguars can live undisturbed. The first such preserve was created by the government of Belize in Central America in 1986.

Deforestation is a major threat to jaguars. When they do not have forests to live and hunt in, they die off.

The Cockscomb Basin Jaguar Preserve has become a model for other jaguar preserves across Central and South America. Dr. Alan Rabinowitz helped set up

A sign in the Cockscomb Basin Wildlife Sanctuary in Belize, which is home to the Cockscomb Basin Jaguar Preserve.

the Belize preserve. He also directs the Save the Jaguar campaign throughout Latin America.

Preserving the jaguar can bring in money for governments and private businesses. Tourists pay to enter preserves and to see jaguars and other animals

Tourists pay to get close to jaguars and other wildlife in a private animal reserve in South Africa.

living in their natural habitat, rather than in a zoo. This kind of *ecotourism* could help save many other endangered animals, too.

If we work today to save the jaguar, future generations will be able to marvel at this awesome animal, just as the Aztecs and Mayans once did.

Glossary

adaptation—A modification to fit a changed environment.

carnivores—Animals that eat only meat.

cubs—The young of jaguars and some other animals.

den—The home of an animal.

descendant—An animal, person, or plant that comes form an earlier form.

domesticated—Made suitable for living and working with humans.

ecosystem—An ecological community together with its environment, functioning as a unit.

ecotourism—Travel to areas with the purpose of observing wildlife and being kind to the environment.

endangered—Facing extinction.

evolution—The process of development of a biological group.

extinct—No longer in existence.

42

food chain—A group of animals and plants in which each group member feeds upon the one below it and is in turn eaten by the one above it in the chain.

genetic—Having to do with genes, an animal's basic units of heredity.

habitat—The place where an animal lives, including the living and nonliving things in the environment.

industrial pollution—Pollution that can be directly linked to an industry.

pampas—The vast grassy plains of southern South America.

predator—An animal that kills and eats other animals in order to survive.

preserve[noun]——A place set apart for protection of wildlife.

prey—An animal that is hunted and eaten by other animals.

rosettes—Patterns on a jaguar's fur that resemble roses, with rings that have dots in the middle.

solitary—Living alone.

species—A group of animals that share the same characteristics and mate only with their own kind.

subspecies—A group of animals that belong to the same species but behave and look somewhat different from each other.

territory—An area where an animal hunts and breeds; the animal defends this area from other animals.

Western Hemisphere—The half of the world that includes North, Central, and South America.

Find Out More

Books

Becker, John E. *Wild Cats: Past and Present*. Plain City, OH: Darby Creek Publishing, 2008.

Squire, Ann O. *Jaguar*. Danbury, CT: Children's Press, 2005.

Walker, Sally M. *Jaguar*. Minneapolis, MN: Lerner Publications, 2008.

Websites

Discovery Channel: Jaguars
http://animal.discovery.com/mammals/jaguar/

National Geographic: Jaguars
http://animals.nationalgeographic.com/animals/mammals/jaguar.html

San Diego Zoo: Jaguars
www.sandiegozoo.org/animalbytes/t-jaguar.html

Index

Page numbers for illustrations are in **boldface**.

About the Author

Steven Otfinoski is the author of numerous books about animals. He has written *Koalas*, *Sea Horses*, *Alligators*, *Hummingbirds*, *Dogs*, *Horses*, *Skunks*, and *Storks and Cranes* in the AnimalsAnimals series. Otfinoski lives in Connecticut with his wife, a high school teacher and editor.